There's more
to the Universe
than they told
you in school.

(Somebody left something out.)

AND THIS IS IT.

This notebook contains
The Universal Principles
of the Universe. ☆

☆

You will not be graded on this material
because in life there are no failures
(only challenges unmet)

Open your heart when ready ⟶

To Learn How

The Universe Works

forget everything you just spent your lifetime

learning and consider your rational mind

[Temporarily Closed For Alterations]

No written exams.

LEARN-BY-DOING this time!

Because only with PRACTICE

comes REAL LEARNING.

⭐ **Table of Contents** ⭐

(for people who like to know what's ahead)

Dear Fellow Traveler,

These notes can be a guide to the road Home. Wisdom to some, windthrow to others. It's packed with lively help if you want it. And understood only by ready travelers hungering for the shortcut Home. Where's Home? If you're lucky, look under your feet. For the rest, um, you'll know when you get there.

I took the long way HOME myself. Never mind that more direct paths were available. I searched for better ground believing that the prettiest flowers were off the path.

1

And so I wandered and wandered away from myself, choosing wrong turns in the right direction (*we're all headed in the Right Direction*), and got my Learning instead by trails that led through tough terrain with my Heart nearly trampled before I reached HOME.

Although I had no idea at the time, in a sudden flash of enlightenment later,
I realized that my own spiritual ignorance in choosing dead-end paths would actually turn out to be my greatest asset! Who but me, a former spiritual blockhead, could better guide the similarly afflicted? Who has a better chance of making the message clear?!?

And so this was the Wild Idea that moved me to write these notes: What if I could meet other intrepid travelers (like you, for instance) who are faced with the choice of:

 A. a Lifetime of Joy

versus

B. a Lifetime of Painful Experiences

and help them decide which is the better?

Simple Truths have a way of getting lost in fancy language and Wisdom often drowns in information, so I wrote this notebook Plain and Simple. It's the Makeshift Map Home.

Battle-worn and shop-soiled, it's been through fire and back, but still ready to help. Use it to learn the lessons first, and maybe you'll avoid repeating the Class.

Faraway friends (both known and unknown) are sometimes those Nearest in Heart, so maybe it is for YOU that I wrote these notes. Do you see what I see? Your answer is as near as this question:

Do you wish to learn these Universal Principles to find your way HOME too?

J. Austin♡

Universal Principles

(The Rules of the Game)

Here is something about the Universe that you may not know and is just possibly the Most-Important-Thing-Never-Told:

THERE ARE RULES TO THE GAME

This should be a relief to anyone seeking Sanity and Peace in what sometimes appears to be a crazy and chaotic world. In fact, the Universe has been functioning just-fine-thanks and as far back as Forever (no, really) due to these Universal Principles, or "Rules of the Game."

Never mind that they forgot to mention this to you in school. This is just a small oversight since wisdom and spiritual insight aren't on their list of basic requirements. (Add that to the list of problems with our schools.)

Also, These Universal Principles work all the time. They are self-winding and work round-the-clock. (Even when nobody's looking.) And we are all subject to them. Ministers and criminals too. And just like traffic law, ignorance of the law is no excuse, because even if you ignore these universal principles you are still subject to their truths. (Just because a principle isn't known doesn't mean it isn't true.)

Unlike other laws or rules, Cosmic Principles are universally true and operative regardless of time period, parentage, or what side of the world you live on. They don't go out of style, don't care how much money you have or Who You Know, and don't take sides. They are immutable and irrefutable. So if you violate a principle, don't rely on your smile and a "*But, officer...*" to help you out, because not even the easter bunny will take your case.

The Universe runs on these Principles (or Cosmic Laws of Energy) just like a car runs on fuel to take you in the direction you're going.

And that's PRINCIPLE.

Spelled P -R- I- N- C- I- P- L- E .

This is not to be confused with The Principal, Divine Custodian of the Universe and a popular religious misconception. However, billions of misinformed earthlings and other spiritual sleepyheads believe that the Universe is run by some sort of Principal.

The Reality, it turns out, is far more interesting. And less scary. The distinction being that the so-called Principal of the Divine Kind is believed to have a kind of arbitrary and limitless power. Should you invoke His wrath even for the tiniest of infractions, He has the authority to suspend you, expel you, call your parents, or worst-case-scenario, send you to a hell of a detention, if He chooses. A Universal Principle simply *is*. It makes no judgments. It isn't arbitrary. It doesn't threaten or punish. It doesn't even call your parents. And it has no intention of sending you anywhere you don't want to go. In fact, these universal principles want to give you whatever you want and send you wherever it is you wish to go. To hell and back even, if that's what you really want. This is entirely up to you simply by pressing the button called "*Your Power of Choice*" then trusting the Universe and following your Feet (this is sometimes called *work*).

As a bonus, these Universal Principles actually work. And they don't give a flying fig if you believe in them or not. No payoffs, prayers or promises can change this. And you can bet the family fortune on it, no matter what your religious affliction is. You need only be in harmony with them (notice I didn't say "obey") in order for these principles to work for you.

To understand cosmic laws, think of the laws of aerodynamics: Follow the Principles of Flight and you soar! Spin out of control (get out of harmony with the laws), and all your pleas to the "Guy in the Sky" will not prevent you from taking a nasty **30,000** foot drop.

Ouch!

So to avoid such painful situations, not to mention the thrill of a Life of Joy ahead for anyone interested in discovering how the Universe works, I present the following 15 Universal Principles of the Universe:

I. Principle of Uncertainty

 Or

Maybe, I'm sure?

The Principle of Uncertainty is actually just the Universe's way of jumping out and saying..."*SURPRISE!*" And Life is full of surprises. This is probably so you can avoid a death-by-boredom.

This is not quite as funny as it sounds. In truth, a life of Certainty leaves little room for Excitement and Joy. And while there are those who tackle life with the efficiency of an organized search party, often the greatest joys in life arrive spontaneously and unplanned.

Granted, reason and data collecting have their place sometimes. (*Government work, maybe?*) But if what you're looking for is Complete Certainty in this Universe you had better go elsewhere to look for another game. Because while statistics work well in large groups, Certainty and Numbers are just plain useless when it comes right down to you personally, like for instance when you need to know if your soul mate is staring you in the face or not.

Oddly enough, in the Things that Really Matter in Life it's often a Decision of the Heart♥ that's called for. And for that you can't depend on data. During these times, you've got to flat out make a choice with very little data on hand. The best you can go with in these times are a "Maybe, I'm sure?"

Of course, We never really know for sure if a Thing is GOOD or BAD until later anyway. And later never comes. Only NOW. And NOW. And NOW. And what you thought was "GOOD" today can suddenly turn out to be "BAD" for you tomorrow and then in retrospect actually turn out to be The Best Thing That Ever Happened to you. Maybe. And the earth keeps spinning.

If you took Quantum Physics 101 but test low on rememberability, here's the science spin on this: Heisenberg's Principle of Uncertainty states that "it is impossible to accurately measure the position and speed of an electron at the same time." This just means that you can never really know for sure where any particular electron will be partying, thanks to Heisenberg's Principle, which is just secret science code for "We Don't Know." (What a refreshing approach!)

And just as you cannot predict with certainty what will happen to any given electron in the subatomic Universe, everything in the Bigger Universe (like your life, for instance,) comes together in a way that is impossible to predict with certainty too. This is just another way of saying that Life is just a Crap Shoot.

The best you can hope for are possible likely outcomes. Because in the Universal Game of Life, Life is Uncertain. That's just The Game you chose when you came here.

And just to be sure that you stay in the game, the Universe holds the *Wild Card* and often plays it right up until The Eleventh Hour just to keep things interesting for you.

Your role is to throw out into the Universe clear requests concerning what you want out of life. Then wait, trusting the Uncertainty Principle (*the Universal paradox!*) to bring it to you. *Whenever.*

And frankly, Trying to predict your future or trying to control what inherently cannot be controlled is a losing game anyway.

So why not forget about predicting altogether and shoot for Wisdom instead? (*It has a longer shelf-life.*) Because while Certainty is important in emergencies and immediate short-term pursuits like diamond cutting and brain surgery, don't count on it to deliver in the long range and the Grander Scheme of things. Trying to peer into events not-yet-unfolded (this is sometimes called Worrying) is best left to Central Intelligence of the Divine Kind, being everywhere and all.

II. Principle of Trust

Everything's gonna be quite all right.

You can depend on the Principle of Trust, the Universe's Cosmic Messenger and Delivery Service, to handle the details once your mental request has been sent. The Universe Supply Company has infinite resources to handle any request and is open all night. *(It's a busy place.)* Trust it. It knows what to do and when to do it (See Principle of Right Timing) and no job is too large.

This principle should not be confused with what is known in religious circles as "blind faith" or knowing, well, *"just because."*

Cosmic trust is faith based on personal experience. It comes from your own time-tested direct and convincing experiment. It's like birth control: It either works or it doesn't. And this kind of proof only comes with Practice. With Practice comes Knowing. With Knowing comes Trust.

This takes some getting used to since originally you learned this backwards (faith first) and Practice was not a basic requirement. To use the cosmic principle, remember that even a Master had to start somewhere. So begin at the beginning, because even a tiny ounce of Practice is better than a giant mountain of faith.

19

To apply the Principle of Trust, try holding a picture of your Heart's Desire firmly in your mind and it will always come forth. Except sometimes. And here's the thing: You've got to trust the Colossal Forces of the Universe to throw all its force behind Your One Big Desire.

Then trust it to handle the better-than-the-postal-system delivery details. There is nothing more trusty than a Universe once summoned. And this is the place to ASK. (Call anytime.) The Universe is never rushed or rude. Ask for Support, ask for Guidance, ask for a new car with a sound system and sunroof.

20

Then trust the Process, which is really the same thing as praying only different. Trusting the Process is the cosmic high performance model. Trust it like gravity and it works. Keep one eye open and you might want to consider a less challenging pursuit, like mountain climbing, for instance.

Remember that anyone can trust when their bags are full. But it takes a master to trust when they are empty. Some get it. Some have to work at it. So when you're out of bananas, remember to practice. Because a few years out of practice and even a master can get rusty.

Unfortunately, this kind of cosmic trust is rarely demonstrated anymore. In earlier times it might have restored to health entire cities from the Plague. But it's been downhill ever since. And this is why Cosmic Miracle-Making has fallen on hard times. There is a gross shortage of masters (one to every couple of millennium is about average) with this kind of trust. Remember, this is Simple.

But no one said it was Easy.

III. Principle of Love

Love will lead you home.

Although many speak of "being in love" very few can define or explain it. This is because love has no extrinsic value: You can't see it, sit on it, or sell it (*although many have tried to peddle the knock-off version*). It is the very stuff you are made of. You had it right once when you were just two-and-a-half and you were Love-In-Action. (*Your parents laughed. They had no idea how right you were.*)

And then you forgot.

Children and Other Advanced Thinkers, however, know that loving Life, Self, and Others are the secret to Real Happiness. They are not embarrassed by this. In fact, the odds against You even showing up here at all are so overwhelming (1 in 13 with 39 zero's after it, or 1 in a quantitative sum greater than all the grains of sand across the scope of the earth) that your very appearance here on earth is living proof that you were created by a loving Universe that loved enough to send You.

That should be reason enough to love yourself.

And the more you love yourself, the more you love the whole Universe since we really are just One Big Enchilada.

The Principle of Love is a form of energy of which you are a part. And although the Universe created Love, it's up to you to put it to good use--each to each--and each of us to the Whole. Because every smile, gesture, and loving thought affects us all. And for every one of us that LOVES, the planet comes nearer to healed. That and, well, because it gives you a good reason to get out of bed in the morning.

There is no situation that can't be made better if you apply the Principle of Love.

25

You don't even have to wait for a crisis, because there is never an excuse for a failure to love, regardless of your judgments of How It Should Be. (*If you can't love it now and right where you're standing... then when can you and where?*)

Love is the unconditional acceptance of What Is. (*What did you think Love would look like? The Bahamas without the jellyfish?*) Love is Acceptance. Acceptance of Self, Others, Life, or the What Is (Whatever that happens to be at the moment). And learning to love What Is, is The World's Biggest Secret. Interestingly enough, the more you love it the way that it is, the more it becomes the way you love it.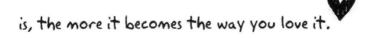

Unfortunately, this is known only by the world's tiniest minority (Children and Sages), who already know the magical effects of Unconditional Love and that the Secret to Life is to collect as many of these moments as you can to Win the Game.

IV. Principle of Attention

What you abhor, ignore

OR

"Sell your clothes and keep your thoughts."

--Thoreau

While it is a lot easier to blame others when things go wrong, actually it's not them. It's *You*. It's your thinking that's out of whack. And bad thinking just creates a lot of bad stuff. According to the Universe's Principle of Attention, what you focus on you create more of.

A bad thought is like a monster that feeds at will--the more you focus on it the bigger it grows

until your life starts to look like a bad movie.
(Think The Rocky Horror show minus the
raisinets.) But if you focus on the Good and the
Beautiful, like a magnet Life brings nice things
closer. This is because the quality of your
Thoughts shapes your reality.

This principle comes to some as naturally as
sleeping or eating. However, for reasons
that would mystify the sane, there are people
who choose horrifying thoughts...like disease,
poverty and *housework!* They would rather
wrestle a porcupine than put their attention
on the Pleasant. Why would anyone choose
horror? *(Is "Crazy" too short an answer?)*

Or perhaps they have too short an attention span for comfort and believe that scary is exciting or that there's fun in being miserable. These are just the sort of people who might enjoy golfing on a land mine.

However, while none of us is likely to escape life's horrors completely, there is no need to overprepare for the event. This is just Poor Thought Maintenance, or ignorance of the Universal Principles. Cultivate a special way of thinking instead.

If a negative thought comes up, there is no need to attack it like a battle commander with a sidewinder (more negative energy) because the Universe will only provide you with more of the same (negative energy creates more of its kind). Instead, why not remain blissfully unaffected by bad thinking? Tell it to go away like an annoying in-law who drops by when you're napping. Or send it positive energy and a Higher Thought right next to it. Plant a flower in the manure.

Here's the good news: Fortunately, these Universal Principles work in a way that is slanted in our favor, like a grading curve for the spiritually challenged (which is the class you're in by the way if you signed up for earth).

In short, one positive thought carries more weight than many negative ones which explains why your worst nightmares rarely come true. It's like a built-in safety net, compliments of the Universe and answers the eternal question, *"Is the Universe benevolent?"*

And whether you believe this to be true or not, you've got to admit that it's a pretty nice way to run a Universe.

V. Principle of Attraction

 Doing at a Distance

The Universe is so simple in design that only children, not-yet-ruined by higher education, get it. Oddly, this Understanding has escaped adults. And here's the simple truth:

We Are All One.

Like a cast of dream characters are all part of the consciousness of **One Dreamer**, we are all part of **One Consciousness** or "*God's Big Dream.*"

Although each of us appears solid and separate, actually this is an optical delusion on a grand scale. We are all vibrating at light speed, very

33

much connected, and made out of the same subatomic stuff (*there ain't no other stuff*). We are all **ONE** energy singing **ONE SONG** (*Uni-verse, get it?*)

All that exists, or has ever existed, is really just a kind of pure energy, ranging from positive to negative, which translates roughly into "GOOD" and "BAD" which happens to depend on which side of the world you live on and Who's In Charge.

Fortunately, because we are all part of **One** Consciousness, reaching out and touching someone instantly anywhere in the Universe in never a problem. In fact, we are already signaling each other subconsciously at subatomic levels where time and distance mean nada.

Even faraway friends who share our same quality of thinking are always only a heart beat away. For the science spin on this, refer to quantum physics (see Bell's Principle of Non-Locality) if you like that sort of thing.

For the rest of us, there is a simpler explanation: Your thoughts automatically attract people and things with a similar quality of vibration or thought.

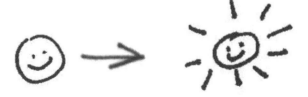

The Principle of Attraction, The Mother of all Principles, sets forces in motion to continually bring like-to-like together like players to a vacant lot. This principle attracts to you what you generally focus on in life, good or bad.

It's user-friendly and ready to assist you, no matter if what you want to bag is a short-legged duck or a husband-to-be. No job is too large, cosmic forces being what they are.

If you are impressed with results here's a visualization experiment to do, otherwise called a "miracle."

To bring something into your life, imagine that it is already there. Then act as if it is. It's like now-you-see-it, now-you-don't magic, except backwards. *First it wasn't, now it is.*

If this process sounds simple that's because it is. But twist it into something that it is not, and it suddenly becomes hard.

And here's the best part: It requires no faith, it's free, and it works.

To visualize, you need to be decisive. Well, sort of. Be clear, but always leave room for the Universe to offer up More or Better. And always make sure that what you're manifesting hurts no one, including yourself. (This is just good cosmic parenting.)

To begin: Choose something small at first and something for which you have very little attachment (nice if it happens, nice if it doesn't). Picture the desired object or event in vivid detail. Make it a mind ride so real you can hear the tires squeal. Now vaporize it out of your thinking. Cosmic translation: Don't worry.

It's a lot like floating. Relax and it's easy. Worry about body position and the first thing you know you're drinking seawater.

And many a miracle was drowned by Doubt.

So what happens next is this: Something or Nothing. If you held your object clearly in your mind then Trust the Process and expect the Universe to bring it to you sometime between now and, say, next Thanksgiving when you are occupied with matters other than miracle-making. Like how to stuff a turkey, for instance.

If nothing happened, do it again. Don't make this a struggle-to-the-death. Relax. So you want to be a Master. What's your hurry?

(You'll be the first to know.)

Miracles were made for practicing. Maybe
you were trying too hard. Or you weren't
clear enough. Or trusting enough. Or maybe your
heart wasn't in it because your mind was focused
on something else, like Balkan history or where you
put the dry-cleaning tickets.

If you did manifest your heart's desire, don't
get carried away by the applause. To a Master,
an object materialized is not a big deal.
It's a requirement. Continue to visualize. Bigger
and better. (Masters get better with practice.)
And only with Practice comes Knowing.

VI. The Principle of Fun

"Life is far too important to ever take seriously."

Oscar Wilde

In the Game of Life, the rule is:

The One Who Had The Most Fun Won.

And laughter is the best way to get there. Laughter can also drive out fear, not to mention that to laugh at life just plain feels good. That should be enough. However, because the truth is sometimes very funny, you'll find that for nearly every life problem there is a punch line. And the lucky ones find it.

This is not to say that everything that comes down the planetary pike is funny, because quite frankly pollution, poverty, disease and terrorism, not to mention your own problems, do not seem amusing. However, being miserable about it is not the answer.

Since reality is shaped by the thoughts that you hold and positive thoughts create more positive energy, the best thing you can do here is to find Humor and Happiness wherever you can ☺ and spread more of it around. Will humor transform the world and cure all our ills? *Probably not, but it could help.* So unless you have a lifetime to spare, you are in it for the duration here. So keep laughing.

VII. Principle of Right Timing

There's a Reason for the Season

All things move in cycles like the seasons, according to its Right Time. And all things in life rise and fall in a rhythmic cycle from our heartbeats to the changing of the seasons. For every action there is a reaction, for every UP there is a DOWN, and for every WIN there is a LOSS, because even nature has her mood swings.

Success comes to those who know when to act and when to be patient, and when the very best thing is to do nothing at all.

There's a time for napping, thinking, planning and waiting. And there's a time for scheduling, controlling, buying and working. A time to sit it out and a time to "Swing, batter batter, swing!"

It's all part of the flow process and often the **WHEN** is just as important as the **HOW**, **WHY** and **WHERE**. So unless you're taking the train to St. Louis, when time takes on a quality of immediate importance, it's best to leave the timing of what you need to The Forces in Charge, remembering that the Universe can stand an awful lot of letting alone.

VIII. The Principle of Integrity

"The greatest happiness in life

is a clear conscience."

--Thomas Jefferson

The Principle of Integrity, once hailed by knights and dreamers, actually works in real life too. That's because in the matter of being decent, NICE never goes out of style.

Responsibility, commitment and compassion build the kind of character reminiscent of heroes and knights, and have the added advantage of a good night's sleep.

Because it is our Self-Worth and not our net-worth that actually determines our outer conditions, in order to develop your self-worth it just makes good sense to refrain from unsportsmanlike behavior (pushing, shoving, and cursing) in The Game of Life and practice instead Kindness and Manners.

This is not to say that it is a good thing to get caught up in all kinds of moral judgments of RIGHT and WRONG. This brings to mind school hall monitors and televangelists. Act with Honor now. Then follow your heart to cultivate spontaneous and Genuine Kindness. Don't wait for the afterlife.

IX The Principle of Right Action

To Do or Not to Do ...That is the Question

The Principle of Right Action, otherwise known as **WORK**, is the Universe's way of handling the inertia problem. In short, there is a time for the deep meditation of gazing at your feet on the coffee table. And there's a time for actually *using* them. Because once in a while even a spiritual master has to come down off his mountain and take care of business.

Sometimes miracles fall right in your lap. And sometimes they don't. And so there may be times when you might actually have to put some sweat equity into a goal in lieu of a miracle, because as Vince Lombardi said, "execution wins it." But you needn't feel rushed on such occasions. You've just got to know when to Let The Good times Roll and When to take Action. Then do it.

What if you don't know what is the best course of action to take and time is running out? Don't worry. You'll know when you get there. Begin at the beginning. Then stop at the end.

Your job is to put out into the Universe clear and heartfelt requests and expect help to show up while you are busily engaged at work.

Be ready to show up for your appointment with Destiny (rationalists calls this Opportunity) and when the time arises take action. Persistence and patience pays off. Just keep your foot on the gas and keep on trucking.

The important thing is that you never give up on the Dream. Break the cycle of Doubts and Fears and do what needs to be done and don't let anyone pester you with the facts.

49

Statistics are for losers (*Vince Lombardi said that too*). And if you don't look out what you are looking for will plow into you soon enough. The hard part is recognizing it when it comes.

The rest is simple mechanics.

X.   Principle of Balance

Nothing ever stays wrong very long

It is the Principle of Balance that is responsible for the solidity of our Universe. By nicely balancing positive and negative electrical energies everything holds together remarkably well. Not to mention that because of this we can all party on the planet instead of dissolving into oblivion.

When you understand the importance of this principle in your own body and affairs, Harmony and Balance in your life is the result.

(That's the good news.) But violate it in the extreme and you've got lots of unwanted side effects, death for instance. For example, even water can kill you if you drink too much of it, should you grossly violate the balance between salt concentration and H_2O.

Unfortunately, people have become so used to extremes that a nice balance can seem uncomfortable. This is boring to people who prefer a good war with themselves. And while peace is not as exciting as raging emotional warfare on oneself, in the long run a simple walk in the woods beats wind-surfing in a hurricane for one's mental health.

In order to maintain a balanced state, remember that working yourself up to an emotional frenzy by using too much force, is about effective as pounding sand, not to mention pushing too hard in one direction will only leave you with the opposite effect.

This kind of excessive force and unbalanced thinking leads to fanaticism and is responsible for giving religion (*a good idea gone bad*) a nasty name.

If you are in tune with the Principle of Balance, you will know that things work the way they need to and obsessive effort and mental struggling will only make a

mess of the whole thing.   Cats understand
this, which is why so few of them have nervous
breakdowns.

Granted, some of the worst things happen
to the best people sometimes, but like
it or not, **The Game of Life** contains both
Success and Failure, Pain and Pleasure.
And that goes for everybody. **No Exceptions.**

This just makes for an interesting and
balanced Universe. Well that, and the
fact that this is **Just How Life Is.**
You can't just have *The FUN parts* version.

The flow of life includes cycles of change. Accept it. (*trees do.*) Prepare for the inevitably of change by not getting too stressed out when negative events occur.

What comes UP must come DOWN. BAD changes to GOOD. And nothing ever stays wrong very long. It's all part of the flow.

So keep humming ♡

XI. The Principle of Synchronicity

☆

Hints from the Universe ☆
OR
There's Something Bigger Going On Here...

The Principle of Synchronicity (or what scientists call *No-Such-Thing*) is the Universe's Guidance Department and Messenger Service. And you don't need a fax, facebook, or voice mail to receive cosmic guidance. The Universe can reach you by license plate, billboard, or song if it needs to. It doesn't need your screen name, password, or ATM code. It knows how to reach you and is available to anyone who wants to tune into this channel.

☆

Synchronicity occurs because all Energy and Matter in the Universe are interconnected and made of the same energy. (Oh, did I mention that before? No matter, some things are worth repeating.) We are a giant web of connections, each part of the web affecting and communicating with each other.

This energy continually attracts energy of a similar kind, whether you are aware of this on a conscious level or not. (Which is why someone like you is reading something like this, for instance.) This is perfectly intelligible to anyone who understands such things.

But to anyone who has never *heard* of synchronicity this is a difficult concept to explain except by way of example.

Synchronicity happens, for example, when you open a book to a page which reads "go for it!" at the *precise moment* you were wondering whether to pack up and move to the West Coast (or the East Coast depending on what side of the country you're reading this book in.)

MIRACLE! to religionists.

COINCIDENCE to rationalists.

SYNCHRONICITY to Those-Who-Know.

58

When a synchronicity happens it often does seem miraculous. The truth is synchronicity has been here all along. It's *you* who's been away.

You were too busy not paying attention to recognize a good hint when you heard one. Or maybe you heard right, but were listening wrong. Like a zebra at a press conference.

As Master of Your Destiny, you get to choose Your Life Script *by the Quality of Your Thinking.* But it is the Universe that directs and choreographs The Big Show arranging for all the people, events, and details in your life to turn up

at the *precise moment that you need them.*
This just makes for a good movie, not to
mention that this sort of participation
between **YOU** and the **UNIVERSE** gives
Meaning and Purpose to your life.

XII. the Principle of Giving

You gotta give what you got

The Principle of Giving flies in the face of the Laws of Economics which encourages you to keep what you've got. The irony here is that the less obsessed you are with getting and the more willing you are to Share and Give, the more you Receive. *(And money unshared only causes legal trouble in divorce court.)*

Although there has not yet been a math invented to explain how this actually works, here's the spiritual spin on this:

You are energy and so is everything else in the

Universe, including Money. They are all the same thing, but in different forms. Giving and receiving are all part of the same flow of energy. If you stop giving you Block the Flow. So to keep the game going you must pass the buck, so to speak.

The Principle of Giving is a very hard concept to put into practice though when you're operating under a terrible time pressure because you're out of granola and you've got to sell the goat to pay the back rent. Still, your cash flow problems are no reason not to put a workable principle into effect.

Granted, while it would be nice to know for sure whether this principle will fly before you give away your last banana, this is no excuse not to. Everybody's got something to give.

There's a free market exchange of Love, Support, Time, Prayers, not to mention cold cash. And those with the least have the most to gain. So give until it no longer hurts.

Because giving is the Universal Law of Love.

XIII. Principle of Happiness

A lifetime of joy–*Who could stand it ?!?!*

Children, who are ignorant as to the importance of money, beauty, and international recognition, are *born* happy. They don't need reasons to be glad to be alive on the planet and playing in the sunshine. Left in their natural state and without adult interference, they would sing like the birds and soar with the wind.

Grownups, who are more loster than you thought, are an entirely different species when it comes to unbridled joy. In fact, once they acquire all the privileges of adulthood, they immediately do everything they can to limit their capacity to experience happiness.

They believe that happiness is where they are not. Somewhere between retirement and over-the-rainbow.

Strangely enough, some people even go to a great deal of trouble to avoid it entirely. Not that they might not want to be happy sometime later in the future (the afterlife, maybe?) just not right now. (They're too busy.) Too many happy days in a row and Perfection becomes dangerously close. "Who pays the check and when is the cutoff?" are questions that plague the happiness-impaired, who get about as much happiness as they are willing to tolerate.

If Fear of Happiness is the symptom then anhedonia, diagnosed by the British Medical Association (no, really) is the disease. This ailment results from the terror brought on by the threat of Impending Happiness.

For those afflicted, the idea of having one's dreams coming dangerously close to fulfillment, which some believe acceptable only in heaven, can prove terrifying right here on earth and right where they are standing, in fact.

People that are afflicted with this malady are people who are low on the scale of Self-Love.

66

They believe that they deserve to lead a life of misery and anger. Some, however, have extended their field of tolerance for happiness and manage to lead lives of the Merely Unsatisfied. Still others who sit on the Bell Curve of Happiness manage to keep it in check. However, their Happiness-Discomfort-Index sets off an alarm when something nears the point of *too-good-to-be-true.*

Fortunately, there are others, however few, who lead happy lives because they believe they deserve to. (*They don't need reasons.*) If you ever find yourself stuck in an unhappy-place-of-mind, it helps to remember that Life has Meaning and Purpose. (*Your very appearance here on earth suggests that.*)

Think of The Bigger Picture.

And Remember Why You Are Here.

XIV. <u>The Principle of Acceptance</u>

If you want to feel great, feel grateful

For reasons not entirely apparent, many otherwise clear-thinking people fail to understand that What is, IS. They refuse to accept that Life is simply the Game of **NOW IT'S THIS/ NOW IT'S THAT.** And that it just makes good sense to let what happens happen.

The truth is, Life can't be any other way than WHAT IS. This is because WHAT IS already is Wonderfully Perfect. Well, maybe not so much Wonderful as it is Perfect. ♥

The Perfection lies in Life giving you exactly the learning experiences that you need to get to a Higher Level of Learning.

However, most adults, without benefit of the natural wisdom of children who are born understanding WHAT IS, believe that the Universe needs fixing. In truth, Reality is all right. It's YOU who needs some adjustment. It's Your Attitude that needs adjusting in order to harmonize With The Way Things Are.

Nevertheless, there are those who insist on fixing. And frankly, fixing works just fine in the short range. Emergency appendectomies, for instance. But in the long range and Grander Scheme of things, fixing by struggle and effort just doesn't deliver.

In fact, regardless of how it appears to you on The Late Night News, the Universe has been doing a fine job, doesn't need fixing, and has been running things for The Good of the Whole, for a long, long time--as far back as eternity and without your help, thanks.

This is cold comfort, though, if you are the one left without a seat in the Universal Game of Musical Chairs. But that's what keeps the game going and makes it fun for everybody. Nothing personal, but that's what games are for.

For every World Series winner, there's a pitcher who blew the game, because when somebody wins, somebody else loses. Like chess, tennis, and being voted off the island. If it were otherwise, winning would lose all meaning. And winning all the time is not only impossible, it's boring. So relax. Everybody gets a chance to dance.

Life is the Learn-As-You-Go space-time game with the Number One Rule being that you must accept WHAT IS. You can't just take the diamonds and some ripe avocados.

So step up to the plate and declare yourself in play, always remembering that the Important thing is that you come down on the side of Wisdom, Truth and Kindness.

Acceptance, however, does not mean happily enduring pain and grief. This is best left to martyrs who have cornered the market on suffering. Acceptance just means that while it is fine to desire something, your happiness should not depend on it.

Shoot for Preference instead. Clinging and obsessive desire only lead to frustration and nervous breakdowns.

Okay, so your life is no bed of petunias right now. Prefer something else, while accepting WHAT IS for now, at least. Life changes and flows. Practice Acceptance and Trust the Flow.

The sure way to win is to make it okay to lose. It's just good gamesmanship.

XV. The Undiscovered Principle

The Value of Not-Knowing

Without The Undiscovered Principle this notebook would be a finished book. And a Finished Book With All The Answers comes dangerously close to being called Absolute Truth. The Danger of Absolute Truth is that there is nothing left to Know or Discover. The Universe is one Living, Loving, and Growing System with plenty more learning left to know. More Undiscovered Principles! Thought-communication! Time-travel! Life-extension! Who knows? Them? (Who's them?!?)

New masters and mystics, who are regular folks like You and Me, are born everyday! The Universe is a Big Place. There's room for everybody! So let's leave room for discovery in this expedition we call OUR LIFE, and be unafraid of the unknown. Let's know that we Do Not Know. Because if you believe that you KNOW just because you got all your ideas secondhand from "THEM"... there is nothing left to find. Not to mention that to be willing to die for an idea that was somebody else's to begin with, is just plain pointless. Even if it *is* comforting.

If you want Comfort and Security, move in with your parents! Call your therapist! Buy a recliner! The list is endless. But this has never been the way of Seekers of Real Wisdom, who are known by their readiness to risk Comfort and Security for Freedom and Truth. This is because Seekers and other Free-Thinkers know that Truth is not for the timid. It takes courage to give up old beliefs. Still, given the options of truth, delusions, or Maybe-I'm-Just-Glad-I-Don't-Know—TRUTH is best. Because traveling the way of truth, which is really a journey and never a destination,

eventually

leads

HOME.

P.S. Whether you bought this book in a store, or received it in the mail, or found it under a pile of rocks, it probably landed in your hands because it was Meant To.
(See Principle of Synchronicity). Maybe it was simply because it was something that I needed to write and something you wanted to hear.

Also, this book was Self-Published which just means that you don't have to go through a Big Publisher to share your thoughts and experiences with its author, which is me, J Austin at gottalottaheartcards@gmail.com

 Or visit my website:

www.gottalottaheart.com

This book was once left by "accident" in a public place and then found by Someone Who Momentarily lost their way "Home." After reading it the Person Who Found It was from then on "inspired to create new possibilities in life."

If after reading this book, you too are inspired to create a new and joyful life for yourself, leave it in a public place for someone else to find. Perhaps it will change their life for the better too.

Pass this book forward by adding your name to the list:

_____   _____
(your name)   (where I found this book)

_____   _____

_____   _____

_____   _____

_____   _____

_____   _____

_____   _____

_____   _____

_____   _____

_____   _____

_____   _____

_____   _____

_____   _____

_____   _____

_____   _____

_____   _____

iling Instructions:

el on back cover

of book down

post office

Thank You!

Made in the USA
Middletown, DE
13 July 2019